POETRY ESCAPE

Break the silence,
tell your truth.

POETS FROM THE NORTH

Edited By Megan Roberts

First published in Great Britain in 2019 by:

Young Writers
Remus House
Coltsfoot Drive
Peterborough
PE2 9BF
Telephone: 01733 890066
Website: www.youngwriters.co.uk

Book Design by Spencer Hart

Softback ISBN 978-1-83928-011-5
Hardback ISBN 978-1-83928-012-2
Printed and bound in the UK by BookPrintingUK
Website: www.bookprintinguk.com
YB0419BZ

FOREWORD

Since 1991 our aim here at Young Writers has been to encourage creativity in children and young adults and to inspire a love of the written word. Each competition is tailored to the relevant age group, hopefully giving each student the inspiration and incentive to create their own piece of creative writing, whether it's a poem or a short story. We truly believe that seeing their work in print gives students a sense of achievement and pride.

For our latest competition ***Poetry Escape***, we challenged secondary school students to free their creativity and break through the barriers to express their true thoughts, using poetic techniques as their tools of escape. They had several options to choose from offering either a specific theme or a writing constraint. Alternatively they could forge their own path, because there's no such thing as a dead end where imagination is concerned.

The result is an inspiring anthology full of ideas, hopes, fears and imagination, proving that creativity really does offer escape, in whatever form you need it.

We encourage young writers to express themselves and address topics that matter to them, which sometimes means exploring sensitive or difficult topics. If you have been affected by any issues raised in this book, details on where to find help can be found at: **www.youngwriters.co.uk/support**.

CONTENTS

THE POEMS

The Word That Nobody Wanted To Hear

The word that nobody wanted to hear.
No matter how many times I whispered it in their ear.
You might think that it is absurd.
Why would a little girl even need to know about this word?

The word describes the pungent smell of the hospital floor.
And the things you see as you walk through the door.
It describes the machine's permanent beep
And the child's innocent weep.

A word which describes so much sickness and pain,
Won't care about your name.
The word described me for a bit.
But I knew that I should never quit.

The word broke my parents into floods of tears.
Knowing that I would have to face many fears.
They knew that having no hair.
Was going to cause people to stare.

Though life goes on at the oncology ward.
Where I am never bored.
My friends and I giggle and play
To try and keep that word away.

But, sometimes, that word makes sadness come along.
So we cuddle up and keep brave and strong.
That word I don't regret
Because all the people who saved me, I will never forget.

Even though that word left me with more than a bruise and a cut
I can definitely say that I kicked cancer's butt.

Charlotte Dawn Crowson (14)
Bridgewater High School, Appleton

Escaping Racism

Black, white
It isn't what you are
It's who you're labelled by
We are all as one
Slavery was a fact in history
Blacks were slaves for whites
How did that work?
Your skin colour doesn't represent or show who you are
It shows how weak the racist is
Your personality isn't your skin
It's deep down in your heart and soul
That matters the most
Blacks and whites
Had different rights
But why? What is different?
Life isn't about hatred and fear of others
It's about understanding that we are all sisters and brothers
Blacks were discriminated against
The segregation blacks faced was sad
The rule that was placed was bad
Love each other, respect each other
Love your neighbour as you love yourself.

Jasmine Karen Griffin (12)
Burscough Priory Academy, Burscough

Silent Cry

A young girl
Once bright and full of energy
The kindest and happiest of souls
Now lies there in bed, counting down the seconds she has left to live
She used to have everything:
A family
A life

But now, nothing remains apart from her darkened heart and frail, skeletal body
Her skin is now drawn over her bones
Revealing what she is going through

People used to say she was overweight
That she should eat less

She listened

She doesn't eat breakfast
Because she doesn't allow it
She has her own rules and they are a recipe for disaster
She is creating a game resulting in one thing
Death

Lunch comes around and she plays with her food
Moves it around her plate

Hoping no one will see
Hoping that her friends won't notice

And, by the time dinner comes around, she is being sick with hunger
Barely able to stand

The doctors said that she was faking it
That it was all for attention
Her parents thought it was just a phase
And sometimes even she would think she was fine
But even she knows this is not right
She knows she should eat
She knows that this won't change her bullies

But she reminds herself this is what she wanted
To finally be skinny and to fit into that stupid pink mini dress

She looks in the mirror and sees a creature-like monster
Just without horns and claws
She thought she was fat

She was not embarrassed, just ashamed
She no longer cared about death
She just wanted a life worth living

She doesn't want anyone to help her
Or at least that's what she pretends
She forces herself to believe it

But she knows deep down inside
That she just wants someone to ask her how she is
How she's feeling

One day, she finally gets what she wanted
Someone to speak to her and say that they are sorry for making fun of her as a teen
But she was now an angel
And the people were standing at her feet
Laying down beautiful flowers where she lay
To make themselves feel better about their terrible traits
And blowing out her candle didn't make theirs any brighter, did it?

You should never advise people on how to take care of their body
By telling them how to hate it
Her anorexia was her silent cry for help
A plea for someone to rescue her
But no one heard her.

Caitlin Louise Illston
Emmanuel College, Lobley Hill

Do Something Now

Climate change
A crisis the world has been avoiding
Aggravating
Pushing to the side
Yet what we fail to see
Is the world disintegrating before our eyes
The once cold cities
Now gasp in the sun's glare
The glistening Arctic
Now a brown, reluctant slush
The towering country of China
Now suffocated by the ghastly air
The once majestic ocean
Now haunted by the saddened species looming in the blackened waters
Heaps and heaps
Piles and piles
Mountains and mountains
Of unusable rubbish scatters the planet
Destroying habitat one by one
Weakening the Earth until it becomes no more
Act, don't accept
Stop, look round
Now it's time to make a change
Do something now.

Maia Stovold
Emmanuel College, Lobley Hill

I Am Not Beautiful

Every day you wake up with an unbearable urge to look pretty
you slump out of bed extra early and complain in your thoughts
about the endless hours to spend on painting your hideous face.
You grow an intolerable itch on your canvas that won't go away
unless you want to be the laughing stock of the school
which is not an option.

You put the most expensive, chic thing you own on your stick-figure body
and style your hair in graceful curls to hide your bushy, natural mane.

Sprint down the stairs quickly, you're going to be late again.
then, squeeze your stumpy, strange-looking toes into your older sister's strappy heels
which blood-blister your foot whenever you take a step
but make you a tiny inch taller anyway.
Walk out the door, don't think about wearing a coat,
get your only reliable friend to pick you up
because only losers get the school bus.

And you are not a loser.

Why can't I be beautiful?
Why can't I be myself and fit in?

Because beauty costs.

You arrive at school, starving
all because you couldn't do your make-up in time and forgot to eat breakfast.
Hurry!
Find a group of friends that you don't even like because - heaven forbid
you're not safe if you walk alone

Your 'friends' leave you.
You're trapped.
Students of all years send a storm of patronising stares
heading in your direction.

Your self-esteem plummets.

Every look.
Every laugh.
Every comment.

Down
Down
Down.

After another day of torture, you arrive home.
The smell of dinner and a blur of noises surround you as you run to your hiding place in tears.
You look in the mirror.

Was it my hair?
Did my make-up smudge?
Maybe it was my outfit?

No, it was them not you
because you -
Extraordinary, elegant, kind, smart you -
are beautiful
Inside and out
just the way you are.

Jasmine Margaret Storey (13)
Emmanuel College, Lobley Hill

Exemplum

Scribblings in trenches
found on their cold corpses.
Poet-soldiers and soldier-poets
remembered now for brief moments.

What evokes our pity?
The poetry? The eleventh?
Who were they that died?
I'll think for two minutes -

Two minutes of silence,
for reflection and calm
of those poets left stumbling,
fumbling in harm.

Owen, Sassoon,
Gurney, Rosenburg -
exposed servants
for God's disabled absolution.

Yet peace can be hoped for,
longed for, yearned.
But the peace that will be
cannot be assured.

We hope for a time
when life's sanctity rules all

No more kind ghosts.
No more militant footfall.

For life is precious -
crucial yet cruel.
Still, all I can do today is warn
True peace poets must be truthful.

Patrick Foley
Emmanuel College, Lobley Hill

Our World

Green becomes colourless
Due to our stubbornness
We neglect the facts
Ignore the impacts

This is our world

Our world which is melting
Our world everyone is accepting

Sea levels rise
Whilst we stay stuck under dark skies
Pollution fills the streets
And the Arctic ice retreats

Climate change is endangering us all
We will fail
So no longer will we hear the birds sing
Or hear the roar of the lion king

We are not aware
That the effect we have is truly unfair
But it seems that no one really cares
Look at what happened to the polar bears

Look at the sea
It might not be empty now
But it may as well be

As the sea is filled with plastic
And this plastic traps the turtles
Yet I don't hear anyone say it is drastic

The warmer oceans are becoming a concern
Which leaves us with so much to learn
How can we stop this?

Bring faith back to humanity
And open our eyes to reality
Our world has changed
From Mother Nature, we have become estranged

But green can earn back its colour
No longer will the world be duller
This is our world
This is our beautiful world.

We must fight climate change.

Mary Fowler (13)
Emmanuel College, Lobley Hill

The Concrete Cage

Her surroundings erupted in chaos
While troubled mothers frantically searched, screamed and prayed
Prayed for the safety of their innocent children
Who by now had already been stolen and could have no longer stayed

The once radiant children were robbed
Robbed of much more than just their homes
But their families too, their happiness, their childhood
All of it was snatched away from their small, delicate hands
And the reason why, it was never misunderstood

Wicked, heinous, brutal barbarians
Monsters who stop at nothing to thrive off the suffering and tears
Of once beaming and carefree families
Who were now left with nothing, but their haunting fears

The daily terrors take over their thoughts and dreams
Turning their pure nights into traumatising nightmares
Which linger through the day, allowing no escape
As it seems to them that no one cares

But she promised with all that was left of her heart that she would help
However, now, as the thunders and roars of distant bombs echoed

Her mind was her prison, paralysing her as it had many times before
The concrete cage trapped her in, no matter how much she bellowed

For she had now realised there was no solution
No way to help her loved ones, but just watch them suffer

There was no way out of her concrete cage...

Sarah Alrawi (13)
Emmanuel College, Lobley Hill

Society

We have got into a pattern of treating ourselves as if we are worth less than others
Why?
Is it because of the number of followers we have on social media?
Is it because of how nice our Feed is?
Or even the number of unread messages we have?
We carry around a list of set characteristics and limitations with us because we think that's all we can be

Well, I have something to tell you
You're wrong

We can be whoever we want to be and we should not be restricted by our physical features
Society has created standards we are expected to meet when no one is really the 'perfect' person
We're just made out to be by the number of friends we have or how 'pretty' we are
We hide behind a screen so no one sees who we really are
We hide behind a Snapchat filter so the world thinks we're perfect
We make each other jealous till we're at a point of mental illness

People are scared to look up from the screen because of what the world will think of them
You miss the opportunities you could have had when you restrict yourself with the mobile phone

You miss the moments you can never replace just because of the piece of metal you couldn't bear to put down

But, when you look back at your life when the years have passed
Do you really want to remember years of looking down at the same screen
Or would you want to remember years of laughter and happiness when you broke society's boundaries?
I know which one I would want
Make your decision now
Don't be too late.

Sarah Iceton (13)
Emmanuel College, Lobley Hill

She Was Only Five

Crying, whining, slowly dying
Under the scraps, shaking and hiding
Tears fall down her soft pale cheeks
As she turns to a gap and slowly peeks
To see her father get repeatedly stabbed
And her mother getting violently grabbed
Scarred by this sight, she is shaken and horrified
How revolting and selfish is this genocide?
She lies in agony while her dreams fade away
Far from safe, she knows it's best to stay
With no other choice, she pulls her hands together
Knowing Allah's the only one who can keep her safe forever
Then suddenly, she senses someone coming over
As the footsteps gradually become louder and closer
She closes her eyes and again, begins to pray
Even though knowing she will not awaken the next day
Then, *clang! Thud!* Bombs and bullets all around
She stands, but is soon shot to the ground
As a waterfall of blood rushes from her chest
All she can do now is lay there and rest
She weeps softly and takes her final breath
She was only five and had already met her death

This is just wrong in every single way
There are thousands of people dying each day
All for a cause that can't even be defined

This is not the reason God made mankind
We should all be equal and help each other whenever we are in need
We should be role models, encourage people, be confident and lead
We should love everyone no matter their religion or culture
Because everyone is unique and like no other
We should embrace and be proud of all our differences
As that's the foundation of how our world advances
We are all capable of stopping this violence and terrorism
And all it takes is commitment and a little bit of heroism.

Sarika Scarlett Riffert (13)
Emmanuel College, Lobley Hill

The Real World

This world is a strange place
Full of news and social media
People creating labels and telling us who to be
It is like a prison
And we are all trapped

A phone screen shines light on us like the sun
Highlighting problems
We didn't even think of ourselves
People pointing out insecurities
We hadn't even noticed

Thoughts go round and round
Our heads are like a bomb
Waiting to explode when we can't take it any longer
Powerful, pretty profile pictures
Intimidate us until we can't take it any longer

But it's all in our heads

We think everyone is judging us
Constantly commenting on everything we do
But the truth is
The only person that's thinking about it
Is us

Our phones are like fireworks
They scare us when we are holding them

But once we let go
We have no worries and no problems
No insecurities

Sometimes we have to put down our phones
And engage with the outside world
We don't realise how many opportunities we miss
If we just opened our eyes
And let go of our issues
We would be so much happier

We all take so much for granted
The trees dancing in the wind
The clouds hugging in the sky
Even the sun shines as bright as a diamond
We all must appreciate it

All we concentrate on is ourselves
If we turn off the screen
And put our minds to rest
Our lives would be so much more carefree
And enjoyable

We worry about our appearance
If we have a skinny waist
Or the prettiest and trendiest hairstyle
But what we really have to appreciate
Is all in the real world

Our phones are not the real world.

Ava Curry (13)
Emmanuel College, Lobley Hill

Pollution

Pollution is everywhere
It's in the sky, damaging the air
But even though you may not see
The damage it does to you and me

Pollution hurts the animals and the land
So please lend us a hand
Show us you care
As it's very unfair

Animals are being harmed
With more than just firearms
Pollution is killing their home
People should have known
The damages it would cause
As pollution has dangerous jaws
That devour all things fresh and beautiful
So you'd better grab a pocketful of nature
Before a giant crater takes them all away.

Morgan Angel Gilchrist (12)
Ferryhill Business & Enterprise College, Ferryhill

Grandad

There's not enough happiness in the world to wipe my past away
But it feels like it was just yesterday when I found out my grandad passed away
Grandad, I'm sorry that you lost your battle to cancer
Now I need to think happy thoughts because grief is not the answer
I just want to be able to wake up in the morning and pretend like it doesn't hurt
Now you're gone, we can't be together anymore, that makes it so much worse
On the day you passed, I wondered why you had to go
Because, if you didn't, you'd still be alive and I'd be able to sleep at night
Why would God take you from this planet and leave me behind?
You loved us, the whole family, and it makes me so sad
That my future cousins will never meet their grandad
A couple of months ago, it was your birthday, but you weren't here to celebrate
They say that, when you die, you always make it to a better place
That may be true, but without you, I don't know how I'm going to make it through
And now, I lay awake and remind myself of everything you did for me
If God is real, then how is any of this stuff meant to be?

I loved you so much and I'm never going to get to tell you that
Just to see your face again, I'd go to the moon and back
But, I know you're never coming back
I wish I had my grandad back
I remember going for walks along the beach with you, my dad and your dog, Jack
Everything you do in life, it's got to be for something right?
And now I have to go to bed and deal with the pain another night
I love you Grandad, you're like the best friend I never had
I hope you're looking down on me, everyone, especially on my dad
And I hope he knows that
I would give everything to be with you and see your smile
I hope you come and visit me in my dreams every once in a while.

Jackson McLean
Ferryhill Business & Enterprise College, Ferryhill

My Family

The bond between me and my mam is a funny one
Always talking about health and safety
I reply, "Shouldn't you be saying that to yourself daily?"
Falling over when she's drunk
And talking about a triple bunk
Always being a pain to me
But overall, I love the punk

Next of all, my sister Amber
The one who loves to climb and clamber
Once, she accidentally fell on a rake
And acted like she'd been bitten by a snake
Even though she is a miss
That is why she's on this list

Now my brother Luke
The one who loves his books
The tiny one in the class
And who says his specs are made of glass
I love my brother, so I do
Even though he stinks of poo

Now onto my dad
Prepare for something bad
He loves his beer and his dear
Most of all, he loves the toilet
When he's making eggs, I say, "Boil it!"

I love my family with all my heart
That's why they play the biggest part.

Dylan Place (12)
Ferryhill Business & Enterprise College, Ferryhill

I Hate That Boy

I like school
Well, I did
You see

This boy mentally
Not physically
You see

I hate him
I hate that boy

Just go
Just leave
Please
Just go

He called me names
He made me feel terrible

I hate
I hate that boy
I do

Just go
Just leave
Please
Just go.

Katie Lee (11)
Ferryhill Business & Enterprise College, Ferryhill

Trapped In My Own Home

I am blocked from the outside world
wishing for a normal life
My personal space always being invaded
getting hurt from left to right
Deafening screams attacking my ears
as each day goes by, hoping it gets better
I want to be like the others
slowly freeing themselves from the nest
but every time I try, it's like I forget how to walk.

Ciena Jordan
Ferryhill Business & Enterprise College, Ferryhill

My Emotion

As the prize goes, my soul follows
And, as it floats, I slowly drift
Into my own world
Into my own life
Into my own body
Into my own emotion
I have no place in this world
I have no place in Heaven or Hell
I need a place in my own emotions
I need to make my childhood last
I need to make amends.

Cerys Harron Jones (12)
Ferryhill Business & Enterprise College, Ferryhill

Stereotyping

No one wants to be known as a thief
No one asks for people to be afraid of them
No one asks to be seen negatively
No one wants to be judged based on their appearance
Just think, how would you feel?

Being a different race and therefore being seen differently
Not getting the same opportunities just because of a disability
Being stared at everywhere you go just because you are unique
This is where society needs help to get over this
Just think, how much easier would life be?

Just because someone looks different to you
It doesn't mean that they steal for a living
It doesn't mean that they are going to hurt you
It doesn't mean that their aim in life is to destroy you
Let it go, can't they show you who they are?

These stereotypes are destroying people's lives
They are causing people to doubt their own personalities
People are out there suffering
Just because of one person's upbringing
Think before you speak, make someone's life easier.

Sophie Weston (12)
Great Sankey High School, Great Sankey

Your Thoughts

No matter our race
We've all earned our place
No matter how we've been raised
We've all had our bad days
No matter our identity
We've all got the same entity

Care for your loved ones
No matter who they become
Mentality is the reality
Looks shouldn't tempt your sanity

Be happy with yourself
How you should be with everyone else
They all have different situations
If taken out of context can cause complications

So, consider this
Before you see them as a miss
Can they help it
Or is your opinion selfish?

Are my thoughts not mine?
My friends'? My family's? Forced over time?
It's not the right way
Don't believe what others say.

Laura Hirst (13)
Great Sankey High School, Great Sankey

Social Media

Social media is mean
Mean to little girls
Girls who compare themselves to Instagram models
Models with fake skin, lips and bodies
Bodies which are viewed as a must-have for everybody
Everybody is different
Different in a good way

Instagram is fake
Fake people, fake photos
Photos with filters and Facetune
Facetune deceives people
People who think that is the standard of beauty
Beauty they need to acquire to feel good
Good enough is false
False because real beauty is what they have

Natural beauty
Beauty isn't how you look or your size
Size isn't what matters
What matters is how you feel in your own skin
Which makes you you.

Maggie Burness-Williams (13)
Great Sankey High School, Great Sankey

Stop Bullying

Bullying is wrong
Don't pick on someone
For their skin or race
Don't look down on them as a disgrace

Making people feel bad is wrong
People might think you are cool
And you might think you are hard
But, in reality, there's always someone bigger and tougher than you

Just imagine
Walking into school every day
Kids treating you like prey
People calling you names

Just imagine how hard that would be
Acting like you're fine
But you're not really fine
Feels like there's no one to talk to
Feels like there's no other way but to hope and pray.

Stop bullying.

Adam Philip Green (13)
Great Sankey High School, Great Sankey

Family

Family is one of the important things in our life
They make sure we are always safe
We make many memories with them
They gave us a good life
They help us when we have problems
They make us happy when we are sad

Family are our first friends
They support us until the end
When we have problems, they are always here
When we are hungry, they give us food
Our family will do all to make us good
They work hard for us.

Darwin Lamban (13)
Great Sankey High School, Great Sankey

Social Media

Social media was made for people to share
Photos and talk to friends and to escape from the real world in general
It has a good purpose but yet
It's still hard to argue and disagree with people
And feuds due to small arguments
Maybe due to different views or something even smaller than that
Instead of using it for fun
It's being taken advantage of and going too far.

Grace Snook (13)
Great Sankey High School, Great Sankey

Rain

Rain, rain
Dazzling in a child's eye
Like a reflection of a diamond
Covering the light
Becoming no longer bright
Grey marks the sky
Clouds no longer joyful but sobbing
Rain, rain
Sorrow of plants
Bringing miraculous leaves of the fresh trees
Lime tree
A silver diamond drop
When it splashes on my car
It races to its death
Rainy days are special
Because they crush the devil
But help the angels peacefully
The rain races and it freezes us
To make us desperately happy
The drop splashes on my face as it paces
Each raindrop is a blessing
Slipping, sliding, the kids fall with laughter
Their dreams come true
The sun fights for light
And achieves a goodbye
To the dazzling saviour of life.

Yahya Hameed (12)
Harton Academy, South Shields

Who Am I?

I'm a fox in the wild
Running through the forest
Wind in my fur, freedom in my path
Adrenaline in my veins, revenge in my brain

I'm a raven in the sky
Soaring through the night
Wind in my feathers, enemies in my path
Blood in my beak, my enemies are weak

I'm a lion in the savannah
Lying in the grass
Wind in my mane, a chase in my path
All my enemies frown and now, they are down

In reality, I'm a lone wolf in the woods
Chasing through the trees
Wind in my fur, captivity in my path
Now I'm tired, shots will be fired

In reality, I'm a mouse in the house
Wandering through the carpet
Wind in my whiskers, traps in my path
Blood in my fur, the cat will now purr

In reality, I'm an ant in the park
Crawling through the sand

Wind in my antennae, humans in my path
As they stomp away, I know I'll never see another day.

Rabiah Zinat (13)
Harton Academy, South Shields

Peace

I can see the headlines
But it's just a piece of material.
A piece of material.
A single piece.
Is it the face
Or is it the cloth?
Every second, every minute, every hour
Every step I take I lose my inner power
Horrible, hurtful words whisper in the corridors
Spreading like a cough
Voices in my head and demons too
Telling me what to do
Telling me I've killed innocent people
I know that's not true
Yet we stay strong
Walking in the streets, people stare
"*Beware,*" they say
"*You'll set off a bomb.*"
The holy book engraved in my heart
The protector and the angels are by my shoulder
We will stay strong.

Aneesa Choudhoury (12)
Harton Academy, South Shields

Time Is Gone

Sometimes, I close my eyes to think
I think about my dreams
And how to become an optimist
My future comes
And my dream job is a horologist

I close my eyes
In the hope the rhythm would stop
The sound of deceit and lies
With the tickling against my heart

Betrayal had filled me
With scars engraved on my brain
There were approximately twelve
And they were all still healing
At such a slow pace

Closing my eyes was a waste of time
For every minute just quickly passed by
And nightmares replayed again and again
They lived long inside my head
Now that I lie here in a nervous sweat
I can say I've lived my life wrong, with so much regret...

Humayra Miah
Harton Academy, South Shields

My Poem About Name-Calling

'Sticks and stones may break your bones
But names will never hurt you'
That's what they say, they think it's right
No doubt, they are mistakes

When they call me a geek
When they call me a freak
When they call me a loser
They say that I reek

My eyes fill with tears
And my heart fills with sorrow
My stomach contracts
And my voice disappears

So now, I speak up
And now I declare
Any bully needs help
To learn how to care

We cannot just leave them
To do what they like
But show them how
Sharing can change your life.

Naimie Chrisp (12)
Harton Academy, South Shields

The Lost Place

In the place
Where no one lives
It's quiet and dark
Because it's the lost place

In the dark
Where nothing lies
No animals or people
Because it's the lost place

Nothing there
Except stones
And darkness
But wait, what's that noise?

Sounds like children
Running and playing
Just like it used to be
Families and friends talking, people having fun

Guess the lost place is lost no more
Until one day
Everyone forgets
The found place was once lost

Because it once was the lost place.

Paige Finn (11)
Harton Academy, South Shields

Grey Paradise

There's a hummingbird on the moon
Defiantly flying free
Away from his home
But he always comes back

Zooming through the air, *buzz, buzz*
On his small, grey paradise
Being himself for once
Being himself for once

Playing rough with his friends
Trying to snatch a seed
All gone away for now
Because he's on his own grey paradise

Flying around the dunes
Never stopping for a rest
Watching the sun come up
Someday, he'll return to his own grey paradise
Someday, he'll return to his own grey paradise.

Kieran Simpson (11)
Harton Academy, South Shields

The Forest

The forest has stood there for years and years
With its trees so tall and its leaves so green
When people walk, the sound is *crunch, crunch*
And when the wind blows, the sound is *swish, swish*

In the spring, its flowers bloom
And everyone comes to the forest
In the winter, the leaves fall
And nobody comes to the forest
The forest got lonely and sad
And thought, *have I done something bad?*

One day, some people came
With chainsaws and evil faces
An hour passed
The forest was no more.

Stephen Hair (13)
Harton Academy, South Shields

Lost Voice

He wandered forsaken in a world of his own
He felt trapped inside
He had never had the freedom to communicate
He walked and walked, excitable children ran past, paying no attention to the lost soul
He turned around; strangers violently threw rocks of him roaring with laughter
He paid no attention, he was used to it
Suddenly, he felt a soft pat on his shoulder - a boy.
"I'm here for you," he spoke.

Zak Abdullah (12)
Harton Academy, South Shields

A Whole New Sight

Life is so unexpected
Life comes and life ends
So soon, our generation will expire

So, when it comes to taking chances
Do it, fake it, grab it
Once the day ends, so does the potential new path

Every decision we make takes us to a new future
If you want something, you need to go for it
So, when it comes to taking chances
Take it...

Laura Jayne Ridley (14)
Harton Academy, South Shields

Arguments

We argue
We fight
We have barbecues
In the bright light

We play in the garden
We make things with clay
And wait
For it to harden

We love
We hate
We watch the doves
While we play

At the end of the day
When I get lost
You tell me the way
Without any cost

Friends are free all day.

Ethan Scott (13)
Harton Academy, South Shields

The Mermaid

There was a girl called Jade
No one knew she was a mermaid
She had so many secrets to keep
Of things that happened down in the deep

Deep down in the sea
Who knew what might be?
The ocean is mysterious
Just like me

Under the waters
Blue and cool
The mermaids go
Swimming to school.

Evie Elizabeth Liddle (12)
Harton Academy, South Shields

Is There A Worse Thing Than War?

The sound was deafening
The raging blood falling
It was stomach-turning
I then began to think
Why did this happen?
But then, I wondered too long
They got me
They ended me
But my last thought was
We have to win
Or they'll end us all...

Demi Barrass (13)
Harton Academy, South Shields

Think

Think is a word
Non-living but useful
Think is a thing you do
Before you speak
And before you eat
Everyday things

Maybe others should think
Think about others' feelings
Before words fall out of their mouths.

Charlotte Harwood (13)
Harton Academy, South Shields

My Dream World

There is a world, we just don't know,
Where thieves and murderers don't dare to go.
In that world, we live in peace,
And everyone has love for each.

There is a world, we just don't know,
Where nothing goes wrong, and we all know
Our children can run and play in peace,
And rest our minds, they're safe.

In that world, all people mix
No fights for rights, because there is peace.
No wars, no battles between the nations,
Except respect that takes its place.

In this world, night and day,
Safety, love and peace will play.
We all know though that world to be
Will never take place. Don't you see?

Peace and safety, we'll never know.
Friendship between everyone will never grow.
Why? No loyalty, no trust between us all,
Don't ask why, because I don't know.

My dream world may never be,
But it's a world I'd love to see.

Loren Cunningham (12)
Kepier Academy, Houghton-Le-Spring

Despair?

The wind is howling,
The sky is grey,
All round me is in disarray.

There's a group in the doorway with happy chappies,
Cider bottles and roll-up baccy.
The woman on the corner and her daughter,
Her face full of wrinkles,
Through years of torture.

The rain drips down my weathered brow,
I really feel my true age now.
My days of being a homeless man,
Seem to be of a timeless span.

I long for comfort, company and peace.
Oh how I wish my woes would cease,
So I go on with my burden.
The chink of light behind each curtain,
Reminding me that despair is certain.

Your fate is not sealed,
Your dilemma's revealed.
Through our care and good deeds,
Your destiny is healed.

Annabelle Hope Scott (12)
Kepier Academy, Houghton-Le-Spring

War

Stop war!
Restrain your anger,
And run to find some shelter.

Stop war!
If you keep fighting,
People will keep dying.

Stop war!
Vengeance and sorrow,
Will be longing tomorrow.

Stop war!
It's not worth going through,
When there are better things to do.

Stop war!
What are we even fighting for?

Without war,
No racism or bias.
The world will exist in peace.

Without war,
No dictators or superiors,
Crime will most certainly decrease.

Without war,
No more killing or murders,
The population will increase.

Stop war,
Nothing is worth fighting for.

Harrison Craig (12)
Kepier Academy, Houghton-Le-Spring

A Choice

A friend is like a star that twinkles and glows,
Or maybe like an ocean that gently flows.

Of human ignorance, I am in despair,
For racism is around me everywhere.

A friend is like gold that you should treasure,
A friend is like an angel that is there to guide you.

Words won't hurt me, that's what they say,
Enemies aren't friends they betray.

Some people carry their honour in a flag
And their nationality, they brag.

Friends have no preferences, favourites or allegiance,
They are loyal and trustworthy
And will never leave us.

Millen Jane (12)
Kepier Academy, Houghton-Le-Spring

Breaking The Chains

Society, a black, vacuous mass
That's just begging for us to remove its mask
And reveal it as the parasitic worm
Sucking us dry of individuality and joy.
Forming us into a non-existent mould,
Grasping us in its strangling hold,
Making a uniform unit,
Of faceless, mindless drones.

The only way to stop this travesty,
Help us all regain our sanity,
Is to go against the grain.
Break free of its invisible chains
Be unique, be abstract,
Throw away all concepts of tact.
Be yourself, be errant,
Our conformation to society is not inherent.

Brandon Riley Lightfoot (12)
Kepier Academy, Houghton-Le-Spring

Bridging The Gap On Racism

I believe all races should be equal,
I believe all races should be kind.
All racism should be illegal,
Our unity we need to find.

Whatever the colour,
We shouldn't discriminate.
Even though in retrospect we lacked,
We should now eliminate
All negativity in the world.

Make this our concern,
Even though many won't.
I just want you to read what I have written
And for us all to keep our word.

Let's all forget what has occurred, start again -
Please.
Even if you struggle,
Let's just put the muzzle
On racism.

Finnley Quinn Thompson (12)
Kepier Academy, Houghton-Le-Spring

Monsters In Our Screens

Nowadays, we spend our lives in front of a screen,
Our eyes are turning square.
It wants to have control.

The monsters in our screens want us to obey,
They want us to go insane.
They want to have control.

The aliens inside apps love attention,
They love to be used all day.
They want to have control.

The mastermind sim card behind it all waits,
He needs to be active.
He needs to be in control.

We need to fight back,
Our phones need to be away.
We need to be in control.

Keira Bailes (12)
Kepier Academy, Houghton-Le-Spring

Racism Stops Now

Noises! Noises! Go away.
I want to hear compliments all day,
But as I soar through the sky,
I hear fans saying players should die.

Noises! Noises! Go away.
Bananas thrown makes me want to help out today.
Racism is a real disgrace,
Let's all be nice and wash it away.
We will all have a happier day.

Noises! Noises! Go away.
We don't need you,
We just want to get on with the game.

Noises! Noises! Go away.
And make sure you stay away.
Racism stops now.

Joe Thomas Atkinson (12)
Kepier Academy, Houghton-Le-Spring

Bang! Bang! Bang!

Bang! Bang! Bang!
Ten men down,
Bang! Bang! Bang!
On the ground.

Enemies shoot,
Enemies shout,
"Lookout! Lookout!"

Boom! Boom! Boom!
Bombs explode.
Boom! Boom! Boom!
It's a secret code.

People kill,
People die.
Children scream,
Children cry.

Where's their mam?
Where's their dad?
Life ahead,
Is very sad.

Peace! Peace! Peace!
No more sound.
Peace! Peace! Peace!
Happiness all around.

Hannah Ruth Marley (12)
Kepier Academy, Houghton-Le-Spring

The Cost Of War

War is a disgrace,
It is a massive embarrassment to the human race.
All innocent people crying,
Their families are dying.
All around the world,
More people are lost.
At what cost?

War is lost and is replaced with peace.
A lasting truth between nations.
People's homes not under threat.
Hopes and dreams to be met.
A future to await.

Ryan Hall (12)
Kepier Academy, Houghton-Le-Spring

My Friends

Friends will always love you, no matter who you are
Friends are always watching over you, just like a star
Friends are always with you, to make sure you don't get hurt
Friends will never bother you, or push you in the dirt
Friends will stick up for you, they will always take your side
Friends will go back and forth, just like the tide
Friends will always love you, no matter how close they are
Friends will never forget you, whether they are near or far
Friends are always kind, they will fill you up with glee
My friends make me happy, I'm so lucky to be me.

Niamh K Marshall (13)
Lime House School, Dalston

Can Anyone Hear Me?

She decided one day
If no one would change
The future of our Earth
She needs to engage

It's gone too far
And we can't rewind
The future of our Earth
We can't dismount

The climate will change
One way or another
The future of our Earth
No turning to Mother

Nature will die
All thanks to us
The future of our Earth
No time to discuss

On strike from school
She decided one day
Some things are more important
Than getting your own way

When will people realise
Our future is almost gone

Can anyone hear me
Is my microphone on?

Julianne Littler (13)
Lime House School, Dalston

Right Or Wrong?

I only smile when the sun shines,
I only cry when it rains,
We need to see fun and laughter,
Not a world full of pain.

Don't deny it,
We won't buy it,
Our eyes are open wide,
Please don't fight it,
Be united,
Divided by both sides.

Is it right? Or is it wrong?
Should we fight to end all wars?
Is it right? Or is it wrong?
Have we all got short-term memory loss?

Lest we forget, help for heroes,
Have the times passed us by?
We need to feel more compassion,
And not bombs fall from the sky.

Don't deny it,
We won't buy it,
Our eyes are open wide,
Please don't fight it,
Be united,
Divided by both sides.

Is it right? Or is it wrong?
Should we fight to end all wars?
Is it right? Or is it wrong?
Have we all got short-term memory loss?

Suranne Pauline Jefferson (12)
NET: North Shore Academy, Stockton-On-Tees

Sun Shine

All in the boat,
Floating, drifting, moving forward.
Years of drifting together,
All of us.
Under the sun's shine.
All of us move in unison.
The sun's shine is blinding.
Under the shine, all is bright.
All is good

And,
Without warning,
Under the sun's deception,
The boat is tipped.

Water gushing in.

Can't breathe.

Overwhelming.

They're leaving me, they're leaving me.
Why are they leaving me?
Years of drifting together
Really meant nothing to them?

Drowning.

Hopeless,
I let the water seep deeper,
I let it take me.
Why would it matter anymore?

I let the darkness grow,
I let it take me,
No one to save me.

All alone...

Suddenly,
Through the blue water,
You were there,
Floating, drifting,
Moving forward in my direction.

Abbie Leigh Simmons (16)
NET: North Shore Academy, Stockton-On-Tees

Testing...

It's meant to be silent.
But I can hear everything.

The flicker of paper
The whispers of children
The shouting of teachers
The clicking of pens.

There is even more.

The whoosh of the wind,
The clapping next door.
The, 'I'll put this answer,
but I'm not too sure'.

Who else hears these?

The complaining for silence.
The zipping of cases.
The, 'I told you to stand,
stay in your places!'

But then we hear these.

The turning around
to rest our sore necks,
The looking back down to our desks.

I know I have eyes,
but I need to check -

where are the men,
who help fix our tech?

Beth Hillman (13)
NET: North Shore Academy, Stockton-On-Tees

What If?

What if what you said didn't get to my head
And I simply brushed it off instead
And my mind wasn't satisfied with what is fed?

With your finger, you slide my worth,
What has happened to this earth?
You decide whether I'm satisfactory
Compare me to society,
Like I'm being deported from a factory
Searching for my flaws,
Then comparing to the laws
That were drilled into your head
And scratched by mighty claws

But what if it didn't get to my head
And I brushed it off instead.

Ella-Faith Ezra (13)
NET: North Shore Academy, Stockton-On-Tees

Tears

Tears roll down her face
Why can't she just go at her own pace?
Working seven days a week
No wonder people call her weak

People say she's not healthy
Just because she's not wealthy
She just wants to start her life
But she doesn't want to part her life

Tears roll down her face
She just wants her own place
She just wants to be pretty
And to live in the big city

She doesn't like the tears on her face
Just as much as the fears she has to face.

Serenna Saunders (12)
NET: North Shore Academy, Stockton-On-Tees

Verbal Bullying

What you call me should only be my name
Not something rude just for class fame
Whatever you say isn't my identity
Whatever you say isn't me

I shouldn't go home crying day after day
Telling my parents about the horrible stuff you say
I shouldn't be scared for the day ahead
When what I want to do is hide under my bed

Why make fun of people for who they are
Making them feel down and saying, "You won't go far."
Telling me everything I do is bad
Then coming home every day feeling sad

Saying horrible stuff about me to your friends
Then they laugh and laugh and it just never ends
Why treat me like a baby and like a small child
Saying everything I do isn't worthwhile?

Saying mean things about my friends for who they are
Angering them and wanted to tear you apart
Lying about the 'great things' you've done
Making fun of others and making their lives less fun

You may think they're just words, but they're really not
Making my stomach turn into a knot

You think it's okay to call me names
Then, all of a sudden, I get blamed?

How long until you realise
That breaking me isn't a prize
Whatever you say isn't my identity
Whatever you say isn't me.

Emily Scott-Norton (12)
Range High School, Formby

A World Full Of Plastic

"It's only one bottle," billions say
Bottle after bag, we throw away
Straws with our drinks for only one use
This planet can't take much more abuse

A quick trip to the shops, or so you think
Ruining our lives with every drink
Plastic packets, plastic straws
Turtles choking, dead whales on shores

Microplastics cause great harm
You eat them daily, does that cause alarm?
No, it doesn't, your ignorance is clear
300 million tonnes made year after year

Fruit and veg, they have their own skin
You don't need a bag to put them in
You drop a small packet, it's not a disaster
Except you are destroying the world even faster

So, when you next complain
About a soggy paper straw
Just think about a future
When the world will be no more.

Amelia McIntegart (13)
Range High School, Formby

It's Okay To Be Different

Freak
Weirdo
Strange
Stupid
'That's her name!'
That wasn't her name
'That's his name!'
That wasn't his name
LGBT
They aren't treated the same
They are called different names
People can love who they like
Not who their parents like
Not who their friends like
It's their affair and you shouldn't care
I didn't say it was simple
But it's your choice
It's okay to not be okay
It's okay to be different.

Molly Elizabeth Large (12)
Range High School, Formby

Everyday Fears

I have a fear
I have a fear that takes over my life
The fear makes me scared
The fear stops me from doing things

I have a fear
My fears are all around
I want my fears to go away
I want to live again

I have a fear
My fear is dogs
They're everywhere I go
I want my fears to go away.

Yasmin Toomey
Ridgeway High School, Prenton

Break The Stencil

This world just seems so organised
Like writing on lined paper
With all the different stages in life
A mere stencil with boulder-thick walls

What if I don't want to be in a stencil?
What if I don't want to explore the rest of the paper?
I don't need your stupid guidelines
Or your complicated exam paper

In my head, I scream and shout
But I can't do that out loud
I'd be ridiculed, tormented and torn
Even if I tried, I would be warned

"Shut up!"
"Head down!"
"You're only a child!"
These phrases make me want to go wild

What? So I need to pipe down because I'm not on top?
But, when I'm an adult, I'll still have a boss
I'm suffocated by the abundance of society
But all I can do is sit here and look pretty.

Della McBride (13)
St Benedict's Catholic High School, Hensingham

The Endless Hug

Tiny and small, a bundle of joy
People tower tall as they whisper quiet, "It's a boy!"
Stumbling, falling, they catch me in their arms
As I feel the warmth, kindness of their huge, hugging palms

I'm not yet fearless and not yet brave
But my parents still give me support that I crave
I started school today, learning to laugh, learning to play
But my loving mother leaves as I'm forced to stay

I'm growing older, want to be like my mum and dad
With a home and a shelter that they never had
How do they feed me, clothe me on minimum wage?
They let me run free, I'm not locked in a cage

Swearing, cursing, hitting with abuse
I cannot control it, I want to be let loose
Grounding's not fun, they take away what I love
My Xbox, my phone, like seriously bruv!

Time's now rough as I have finished school
Living on the streets, I try to play it cool
No help from my parents as I pushed them away
Living by myself, alone every day

Running to the door like a child from school
Tears come pouring, I look like a fool

I have weakness in my bones and conflict in my head
Every day, I live, somehow I dread

I see her there as a shadow on the floor
She sheds a small grin as she awaits me through the door
Stumbling, falling as I run into her arms
As I feel the warmth, kindness of her loving arms.

Ava Gill (13)
St Benedict's Catholic High School, Hensingham

Ghosts...

We were just there for a trip
We heard the hotel was haunted
But what we found changed us forever
The rumours bounced around like dancers in a ballroom
They were cut short by the lights flickering before leaving
Minutes later, they returned with a new party not far behind
That night, they called our room
And moved things in the cupboard
But we charged on, determined to solve this mystery

We were warned by professionals
But ignored their plea of green
We were advised not to make conversation
But we took the chance and made contact
We took chances and avoided common sense
We provoked the ghosts with treats instead
As the clock struck eleven, they tried to chase us away
But we didn't give up so easily
We planned to stay the night

Our stay at this hotel was certainly strange
But the person we met was stronger
She knew things that normal people don't know
Like who we are and the spirits around us
As we left, she said the final thing
She told us about a forest, hidden from sight

Where witches and figures scare people away
We were just there for a trip
We heard the forest was haunted.

Leah Dunn (14)
St Benedict's Catholic High School, Hensingham

Tragedy

Waves crashing, rocking boats
And terror of sickness.
Dozens of men in a boat
Some shaking with fear
Some throwing up pure evil.
Bullets began crashing against the sea
Then the strong metal of the boat.

Bullets clashing against each other,
Bodies dropping to the ground like loose cannons
Bullets flew around like wasps in the summer.

As men were shot, they were held down
Like cement sinking in and drying up
As it held them down.
They soon entered the skies above them.

Fear debilitated them like a missing leg
Preventing you from standing up for yourself.
Men fell down like domino pieces
There were a thousand men
But, in a matter of seconds
It turned into less than 500
After a couple of months, war was no better
500 to 200, it never got better.

Families were devastated
By the loss of their loved ones
They will never be forgotten.

Molly Parker (14)
St Benedict's Catholic High School, Hensingham

Top Of The Hill We Get

Ping! The bullet clashes with the metal
Sink, the bullet falls into the skin
You will be okay they said
Millions of soldiers lay there, pretty much dead

Move forward, open fire, gas
The shouting never stops from commands
To the yells coming from the brave men
Who sacrificed themselves

Top of the hill we get
My best friend behind that I just left
Surely this must be it
My sergeant calls, then sadly gets hit

End of story, well, that's what they -
"Fire!" ugh, that's what they say every day
Bang! Is this the end?
Me and a few men
Maybe about ten

We made it to the end
The fields, gruesome and gory
Now we can finally say, end of story.

Ella Bristoe (14)
St Benedict's Catholic High School, Hensingham

Monaco

Eyes are the windows to your soul
Goodbyes are the hardest of them all
One person leaves, another comes
When you arrive, no one knows

A mission awaits for me to complete
That will leave you hanging on the edge of your seat
So hold on tight and don't let go
As we head down the road to Monaco

Screams of children fill the night
As the man in black must fight
So my hand gripped the gun with all my might
I had to be the one to win tonight

My helpless body lay on the ground
I couldn't hear a single sound
Chills rapidly raced down my spine
Then I realised victory was not mine

When reality hits
It was time to go
I had to say
Goodbye Monaco.

Courtney Nicholson (14)
St Benedict's Catholic High School, Hensingham

Final Letter

As my dying comrades
scream and moan
I have a rifle in my hands
all alone

The rotting stench makes me sick
I need to escape
think
quick, quick!

I move my head
from side to side
I need to find
a place to hide

I set off
and start to jog
around rotting bodies
and disgusting bog

This isn't what I signed up for
for gruesome sights
and bloody gore

I wonder
where is my team?
I look up
the gas sirens start to scream

I search around my body for a mask
surviving this war is my only task

Oh no! Where has it gone?
my eyes widen as they start to tear up
this is where I die
Mother, Father, goodbye!

Oliver Clingan (14)
St Benedict's Catholic High School, Hensingham

The Unseen And The Unheard

Why can't you hear us
When we're screaming at the top of our lungs?
Why can't you see us
When we were right in front of you all along?
We are screaming, we're shouting
Waving our hands in your faces
What's more important
This dying Earth or these burning places?

What good is a building without a place to stay?
We have to help our Earth, not just run away
We know all these problems
But choose to turn our backs and simply watch our world collapse
What has our existence come to?
I don't want to live like this, do you?
Join me, scream, shout
Wave your hands about
So we can be seen, so we can be heard
And no longer be the unseen and the unheard.

Mary Kirsten Soriano (14)
St Benedict's Catholic High School, Hensingham

The Chain

The chain is a thing that hurts me
The chain is a thing that annoys me
The chain is a thing that haunts me

It hunts you down
It works you out
It finds a way to break you

The chain is a thing you see every day
The chain won't leave you alone
The chain picks at every bone until you have nothing to work with

It picks at your head, it picks at your brain
It finds a way to hurt you
It knocks you down, you get back up and it does the same again

They think they are funny
They are always rude
They find a way to hurt you

They think they are tough
They act very tough
They really try to hurt me

This is the social chain...

Sam Garroway (14)
St Benedict's Catholic High School, Hensingham

The C Word

No one likes to hear the C word
It's nasty and vile and cruel
Just saying it causes a room to go tense
The mere silence for minutes after
It shouldn't have to be said
It shouldn't need to be said
It should just disappear
The lucid feeling when you're told someone you love
Isn't going to be okay ever again
And your eyes sting with anger
There is nothing you can do
Just wanting to scream
Your lungs don't work
You get choked up
You want to run and put your fist through a window
But you can't even move
You are helpless
The numbing pain when you have to smile
And say you're okay
When you aren't...

Evie May Tyson (13)
St Benedict's Catholic High School, Hensingham

War, War, War

The night was dark, the night was dull
Breath and bodies made the room full
Guns and armour on the floor
"I don't think I can take any more."

Smoke and pollution filled the air
We moved on and tried not to care
Trenchfoot and disease were passed around
"Quick! Take cover!" Don't make a sound

My friend suffered where he lay
It got worse almost every day
Hard to breathe, struggled to move
We barely had enough to share our food

Scars, bruises and wounded all over
I hope it's back to normal in October
Now it's time, I have to go
Might be dead, you never know...

Holly Laing (14)
St Benedict's Catholic High School, Hensingham

It's Hard To Say Goodbye...

It's hard to say goodbye
They meant so much
It's as if the plot of life
Just got worse

It's like they're two people
One may be different
One somewhere else
But they're just one for me

I've been with them for years
Throughout all the seasons
I saw them happy, I saw them sad
I saw their ups, I saw their downs

Everything's going downhill
Everything's so sad
It won't be the same without them
Things could get nasty

I've mentioned all these feelings
But there's one more thing to say
It's a shame they're not real.

Sophie Kate Rodgers (14)
St Benedict's Catholic High School, Hensingham

Dragon's Breath

The dragon's breath
A warm, lethal fire
Burning hot like human desire
Over our heads like a warm, loving rain
Only when it splashes you will you not be seen again

The scorched earth is our only reminder
But with this, the world only becomes blinder

The stage I set may seem pure, pure fantasy
But these events outline a stark reality

The flamethrower a weapon only made for killing
But those at the other end were more than willing
To die for their country like any good soldier
For this is the reason many youths never grow older.

Kaiden Bell (14)
St Benedict's Catholic High School, Hensingham

Reality

The strong stench of fear poured out of their mouths
The noise of silence filled the boat
Suddenly, words of terror became commands
Bang! This was now reality

Faces like canvases, no colour, no emotions
Disturbing the sea from its slumber
Enemies firing in all directions
Bodies so heavy, sinking with no escape

Soldiers with no control which fate had decided
The blood attacked the sea as the soldiers dropped one by one
Bodies turning inside out
Trying to save each other
Before it was too late...

Kacie Gillespie (14)
St Benedict's Catholic High School, Hensingham

Her Body

You preach about love
And respect and kindness
You live on social media
Trying to be beauty's royal highness

But you speak about her
And it's why she self-harms
It's the reason that she cuts
Into her legs and her arms

But you keep on at her
As she walks out the door
About her hair and make-up
She doesn't want to live anymore

So, when she cries at night
Whilst you're sleeping in your bed
She never dwells, like you, on Instagram
She would rather be dead.

Isabella Brown (14) & Lara Hodgson (14)
St Benedict's Catholic High School, Hensingham

As I Lay

As I lay, I finally see the peace from war
As I lay, I see the calm after anger
As I lay, I see soldiers returning home
From the traumatic war to the hopeful families
As I lay, I see the crying of sorrowful mothers
As they find the horrific end of their children's fate
As I lay, I can still see shrapnel ripping through the bodies of the unfortunate
As I lay, I can still see bullets whizzing through the sky
Until they finally come to rest
Laying a soldier's mind to rest.

Kyan Willis (13)
St Benedict's Catholic High School, Hensingham

The Pure Souls

At the dawn of the full moon
She came out to obtain what wasn't hers
Wandering the streets, waiting
For the soul so pure

She'd wander and wander for hours it seemed
Until a house she'd find
With an innocent child
Pure as gold

Blood-red eyes
At the end of his bed
She grabbed and dragged the unfortunate soul
Screaming and screaming, yet no one heard
She took him into the raven night
Never to be seen again...

Tiegan Quayle (14)
St Benedict's Catholic High School, Hensingham

God Bless

God bless his heart
That's not in his body
God bless my wounded soul
That won't leave his ghost behind

God bless his last supper
That poured out of his ruptured gut
God bless my thrashed eyes
As I've seen the devil

God bless his legs
That can't carry his praying mind
God bless our shaking hands
As he fell dead

God bless this place
God won't bless this place.

Lucy-Beth Callander (14)
St Benedict's Catholic High School, Hensingham

No-Man's-Land

As our commander stood tall
The silence filled throughout the trench
"Now boys, now!"
The boys rushed into their graves
Cheering with pride
The drumming machine gun's roar
Echoed over the battle-ready chorus
Cheering turned to sorrowful screams
And then a silence of despair

Boys who dreamed for glory died with sorrow
For silence falls in no-man's-land.

Tom Arins (13)
St Benedict's Catholic High School, Hensingham

Evolution

Evolution: the process by which different kinds of living organisms are believed to have developed from earlier forms during the history of the earth,
We have evolved in body and in mind,
Homo sapiens,
But homo is not normalised,
It is forbidden,
Looked down upon,
Pride: confidence and self-respect as expressed by members of a group, typically one that has been socially marginalised, on the basis of their shared identity, culture, and experience,
But what if your pride is tarnished by someone you trusted,
Out,
I had a plan,
A letter detailing my orientation when I thought was a time when I was comfortable,
But rumours grow and suddenly,
Out,
Every day questioned about who I chose to love,
Why?
How does it work?
"Pansexuality isn't real you're attention-seeking,"
"Pick a side,"
"Pick a side!"
"What about straight pride, we exist too?"

Asking for straight pride is like asking for a cemetery for the living,
It is like asking for service dogs for the able,
It is the equivalent of giving medicine to the healthy,
If you insist on having straight pride along with the other eleven months you have to be who you are,
You should have it our way,
Protesters lining the streets,
Hurling abuse at an already fragile community,
Being touched,
Spat on,
Punched,
And even killed
All because of whom you chose to love,
Every day, we move further from equality,
Every day, people like us are killed because of who we chose to love,
But I am still here,
I am lucky enough to have people that support me,
I know who I love,
And most importantly,
I know not to listen to your poor judgements,
To your harsh words,
And the insults you brandish like fine china,
I know that I am small,
But I am strong in will.

Ellis Heywood
St Bernard's Catholic High School, Barrow-In-Furness

Football

When I stepped across that white line
The barrage of grief had just begun.
It sent shivers down my spine.

Why were they telling me I'm black - I obviously know this?
The abuse was coming from my own fans.
The racial noises were a constant humming hiss.

Put the comments to the back of my mind.
Deep down, the talent I find.
As I look up the goal in sight.
The racial abuse I must fight.
Now the ball's in the back of the net.
No racial abuse, what a delight.

Callum Paton (13)
St Bernard's Catholic High School, Barrow-In-Furness

'Weird'

People say, "Stop being weird."
I say, "Weird is the new normal."
People say, "Why are you being so gay?"
I say, "What's wrong with being gay?"
These make me me,
It's okay to be different,
You are your own person,
No one else.
If you want to be different,
Do it,
Do not let anyone
Do it for you.
If they call you names,
Just block them out,
You are who you are,
Don't let anyone change that.

Phoebe Mary Grace Faragher
St Bernard's Catholic High School, Barrow-In-Furness

Backwards

I hate my reflection in the mirror
You will never hear me say that
I'm good enough
I know in my heart that
The number on the scale shows what I'm worth
And that
Being thin will make me happy
I refuse to believe that
There is hope
I am ashamed of my body
No longer can I say that
I am worth fighting for

Now, read backwards.

Izzy Kingston (13)
St Bernard's Catholic High School, Barrow-In-Furness

Rainbow

Differences are different,
It says it in the name,
It comes from all our ancestors,
We all play the same game,
Don't try to be someone else,
Just be like me,
Block out any other hate,
As it will grow through your family tree,
It doesn't really matter if you are any other colour,
Because if anything,
I would choose to be multicolour.

Maddie Williams
St Bernard's Catholic High School, Barrow-In-Furness

Mental Health And Body Image Poem

Allow me to talk
About how I am feeling.
It's part of my life,
A part that I'm healing.
Our mental health matters
And I don't want to hide,
I want to be honest,
So don't worry about asking, "How are you?"
You'll find that I'm human
And you've nothing to fear.

Evie Lyla Downing
St Bernard's Catholic High School, Barrow-In-Furness

Racism

Black, white, yellow, blue
I love you for you
Skin colours don't matter
I don't care if I sound as mad as a Hatter
You're beautiful in every way
Who cares what they say?

You shouldn't have to feel these feelings
They're pulling you in, almost reeling
Depression, anxiety, heart attack
The feelings are piling up, turning into a stack
But remember, even when there's no light of day
I'll always be there to guide you away.

Freya Humphreys (13)
St Chad's Catholic High School, Halton Lodge

Homeless Poem

H appiness is hard to find
O n cold winter nights, we lie there, waiting for death
M ornings come but no hope is left
E very day is a struggle
L onely souls feel they have no purpose
E very day blends into one
S uffering is all they feel
S o we must help them heal.

Gemma Humphreys & Eleanor
St Chad's Catholic High School, Halton Lodge

Dear People Of The World

Dear people of the world.
My name is Adel and I'm a 'terrorist'.
I'm sorry for all the killing, bombing and kidnapping 'we' do,
I know it's hurting you,
But it's hurting us too,
Apologising for something we did not do,
I'm sorry the media brainwashed you all,
I know you don't want to place stress and blame on us.

Do you know what? I am not sorry,
I am not sorry that 90% of the terror attacks are by non-Muslims,
I am not sorry that we created the first ever
university,
coffee,
soap,
and even algebra
I can go on for days.
Every human bleeds red and we don't?
The breaking news that we hear every day about 'Muslims' is fake.

Dear people of the world,
My name is Adel and I am a Muslim.

Adel Al Suraimi
The Academy Of St Francis Of Assisi, Kensington

Your Problems

We have a system that is failing us
Only teaching us to pass
Tears of stress and anguish
Flood each and every class
We wish to learn, achieve, create-
But we are shoved aside and moulded
Into something we are not
No - we are not babies
Confined to old-fashioned cots

You call us arrogant and audacious
Scornful and selfish
But we couldn't care less about the labels
You give us
No matter how hard
You shove them down our throats
We are a generation of:
Technology
Fake news
And activism
Don't tell us what to do
When you don't understand us
To go outside
When it's smoke from your generation's factories
That darkens our blue skies.

We hear you but we cannot listen
(I have too much revision to do)
I have no time to listen
To the problems you blame on us
I don't have time to be what you claim
You forget we all are teenagers once
So I'm lying where you've lain.

Martha Hornett
The King Edward VI School, Morpeth

Our World

Animals are scared
Trees are lying
Ice melting
The poverty is high
Is this the last goodbye?
Ice is melting fast, fast
This is the last
Trees we need for air
But what about that bear?
No one cares, no one
Soon we will be gone
We need to help, no one
Soon, we will be gone
We need to help, if we don't
We will be in the same boat
Listen to the kids, we all know
'Cause we don't want to go
We love the world today
Because we want to do things the right way

Animals are happy
Trees are everywhere
Ice is hard
Poverty is gone
This is the world I want
What about you?

Phoebe Lovidge (13)
Walney School, Walney

Breathe

Breathe, just breathe
Let the words come, but don't let them sink
Build a wall, let nothing in
Breathe, just breathe
Count to ten
Count to twenty
Count to one hundred if you have to, just don't let them see you break
Breathe, just breathe
Take it in, blow it out
Let them see you strong, don't crumble
Breathe, just breathe
It won't be too much
Breathe, just breathe
Breathe, just...
Brea...
Br...

Lucy Hanrahan (14)
Walney School, Walney

Tomorrow

Today, we cut down forests for paper and wood
And are ruining them in the process
We'll sort it tomorrow
Today we poison the air with the increasing amount of CO_2 from the factories
We'll do it tomorrow
Today, we dump our litter in the ocean,
Killing the sea life in the thousands
We can fix it tomorrow
Today, we overheat the world which causes the odd droughts
We'll do it tomorrow
Yesterday was the past, we used people instead of machines
Swords instead of guns and fire for light
Today is now, we destroy forests, pollute the ocean
Poison the air and corrupt the land
Tomorrow is the future, it won't change until we change the present
We're not doing that
We cannot keep waiting to do stuff tomorrow
If we don't act today, there will be no tomorrow to fall back on
It's not fair to make the people of tomorrow fix our problems

Today we need to fix what we've done for
The present
The future
Our home

We need to save it because, if our home dies
We die with it
The future suffers for our actions
We need to save today so we can see the sunrise of tomorrow.

Nathan McDonough (12)
West Derby School, West Derby

Escape... While You Can...

Society is balancing on a tiny, thin blade
One little movement could plummet you over the edge
Earth used to be green, calm and zen
Now, it takes the smallest wound to ruin a family for life

It's only one tiny moment, short, useless and destructive
Except, it ruins homes forever, obliterates feelings
It's demonic, it's devilish and what satisfaction is given?
All for nothing, innocence demolished in a blink of an eye

You could be happy, successful, on top of the world
For it to be gone in seconds, no goodbye hugs
And it's mostly in gangs, hiding in alleys, kids' lives vanish before they've started
They can't see a way out, no one to talk to, alone

So, how do you feel? Guilty? Scared? A victim? You should
If you're a part of this problem, ask yourself why
The knives aren't worth carrying, a wound too deep
So put down the knife and escape while you can
Because some people can't and it's too late.

Lewis Loftus (13)
West Derby School, West Derby

Pain!

It's the worst feeling in the world
Most people feel it
Some are so bad
They end it all

People say, "Just get on with it."
They don't know the pain
They can speak to somebody
They don't have the demons pushing them down
Telling them they are worthless
Demons wanting you to end it all
It can all be done in a flash

It can all start with a word
'Fat', 'ugly' or 'meff'
It can destroy somebody
You can't see the cuts and bruises that it left
But it is slowly breaking somebody down
It's like a hammer breaking through glass

No matter what, the people are pushed down
They come back even stronger and will become the best!

Harry Dermott (12)
West Derby School, West Derby

The Labyrinth

There's no black
There's no white
I know we're all in a haze
But we can get out of this maze

We gonna turn a right
We gonna keep up the fight
We're not gonna back down
So don't you dare frown

"Turn a left," a black person said
"Turn a right," a white person said
So we ended up splitting
And oh how we walked away ashamed

Escape is what we wanted
Separation is what we got
No one could find their way out
In the end everyone was left to rot

We should've stuck together
Travelled as one
But we couldn't break our tether
And now we are going

There's no black
There's no white

There's no fight
There's no right.

Pape Mbaye (13)
West Derby School, West Derby

I Forgot What My Poem's Called

It hits you hard like tripping and falling - unexpected
and scary
It's like someone has thrown a brick at your head and
you forgot
You forget your family, your friends, your loved ones
You forget the places you've been and the places you
want to go
You forget everything

You get put down, thinking your time has run out
Thinking it's your time to leave this world
Thinking it's your time to go to a better place
You have to stand back up
Don't give up on a life that isn't yet gone
Don't give up on the time you have left to do what you love
So, stand back up and live your life
Until it actually is time to go
Live until you are done.

Charlie David Watson (12)
West Derby School, West Derby

Anxiety

Anxiety, do you know what it does to you?
Can you make sure that you will get through?
Don't let these demons get inside of you
'Cause it will be hard trying to fight them too
Trying to find them while they're setting flames inside of you
Not knowing what to do
Not knowing whether to speak out
Or keep it all gathered up inside you
But you have got to speak out to someone
To get these people out of you
How it's their turn to fear you
Not knowing the damage they have caused inside of you
Now they know what they have done to you
Now they're looking for another victim to do it to.

Johnpaul McNally (13)
West Derby School, West Derby

The Pain

My pain may be the reason for somebody's laughter
It may also be somebody's source of entertainment
Never do a wrong thing to make a friend
If you do, the pain will never end
Bullying breaks people like a hammer breaks glass
If you break someone, the impact will last

I want to share this poem with you
Because some people don't know it's true
Every bad word or action you say or do to someone
Impacts the rest of their life until the day they die
Some people even take their own life from the reach of the Earth
They take their life because they don't know what it's worth.

Sean Donnelly (12)
West Derby School, West Derby

Life Is Not Short!

Lost in a world of darkness
All you can think of is family and friends
Gone forever
There's no turning back when it happens
Think harder
Think greater
Think beyond

Suicide
Around one in five teenagers around the world have suicidal thoughts
But life is not short
We have everything and anything
But we don't use it
We take it bit by bit
And don't think ahead
Sometimes, we cry in our bed
Life is not short!
Don't waste it, use it
As a ticket to freedom
And make the most of it
Life is not short!

Johnny Tierney (13)
West Derby School, West Derby

Depression

Depression is like a shadow, it follows
It destroys people's lives, making them full of sorrows
Covered up with fake personalities, that's a fact
People being forced to wear an artificial mask
It is unstoppable, tearing people apart
Making them believe they have no heart
Suicidal feelings corrupt their souls
Leeching on them until they grow old
This needs to be prevented, stopped and ended
Our mind needs time to recover, so defend it
From negativity and all bad things
All the bad things that depression will bring.

Shaun Veach (13)
West Derby School, West Derby

Social Media: The Issue

My eyes obsessing over a blank screen
Looking at the likes, I hope no one's mean
Forcing me to put on a mask of happiness
When really, lurking inside is the emptiness
Bad decisions awaiting at every turn
Causing me depression, when will I learn?
How can I fix the mistakes I've made?
Chill out, relax, take cover in the shade
I don't think I can, I'm in too deep
I hate this feeling, I can never sleep
I wish somehow, I could make my life easier
Now, these are the problems with social media.

Luca Burnett (13)
West Derby School, West Derby

Shooting Range

Being bullied is like being in a shooting range
And you're the one being shot at
You have no gun
No bullets
But they have a clear view
Then they pull the trigger
With their sights on you

The bullet goes through
Better than staying with you
If it stays, the words do too
They don't care if it hurts
If they hit their mark
The people you love come to check on you
Bulletholes through and through
You cover the holes
Your loved ones think the shooter missed their mark.

Joe Gossage (11)
West Derby School, West Derby

A Wartime Soldier

He might be displaced
But God only knows what he's faced
People call him a soldier
But he calls himself a killer
We see their medals
But to him, it's a piece of metal
He might have wrecked families
But destroyed his own
He might be lonely
But he's not the one and only
Guns he may have used
But he didn't intend to abuse
He's an invisible vision
But it wasn't his decision
He might stand out
But he's a background character.

Jack McGrath (13)
West Derby School, West Derby

It's Not Funny

Stop calling me this, stop calling me names
The bullies all think it's fun and games
They do it while laughing, they do it for fun
You can't silence me now, look at what you have done
I'm always crying, I'm always anxious
My life is filled with suicide and sadness
I remember in Year Three, I was called a dummy
It only got worse you see, it's not funny
Some kids just want life to end
So listen to us and the message we send.

Connor Lampkin (12)
West Derby School, West Derby

My Brother And I

Ben, my big brother
He is there for me
From when I climb a tree
To when I fall down
When I'm down
When my emotions are down
He turns my frown upside down
His name is Ben and he is my big brother
I love him
From when I went through tough times
To this day, he is my brother
Suicidal thoughts used to be on my mind
Ben helped because he is one of a kind
My brother and I.

Joseph Stephenson (13)
West Derby School, West Derby

Us

We did this
Us
Humans
Whether it be us
Our parents
Their parents or their parents
It was still us
Us?
Yes, us!
The unbearable litter that scours all floors
The plastic waste that infects all waters
If we don't stop now, it will happen more
What will we tell future generations?
The flowers used to bloom?
Not anymore
Used to swim in water?
Not anymore.

Thomas Bragger (13)
West Derby School, West Derby

Hope

Hope
It's the reason we all wake up
Because tomorrow
Is not guaranteed

Hope is why you eat
Sleep and breathe
Because the nutrients in food
The oxygen in air
And the growth in sleep
Are not guaranteed

Hope is why we work hard in school
Because we hope we will get a good job
Hope is the heart of the world
We hope for tomorrow.

Ethan James Woods (13)
West Derby School, West Derby

World War

It was mayhem
Country fighting country
Men went to fight for their country
And never returned
Bullets flying in every direction
Men died in different countries
Those brave soldiers will be remembered
And there will be one person who I will remember
My great-great grandad
The world should never forget
These horrific four years of war.

Alfie Bryce-Hunter (12)
West Derby School, West Derby

My Life

My name is Scott
I have
lost
people in my life
but
I know
they're still
there in
my heart.
When they
died
half of me
died inside.
Just imagine
if
that half
of
me
was a
fire
and was
extinguished.
Just imagine
Just imagine...

Scott Holloway (12)
West Derby School, West Derby

This Is Me!

Every morning, I lift my head
Some I'm fine, but most I dread

Down for breakfast then off I go
Up the stairs, get ready to go

Ready and sorted, off we go
I leave the house like a timid mouse

We leave the house at eight o'clock
Get to school, my heart will drop

I walk around the car and give a high five
To my wonderful mum who sits inside

Through the gates with my brother
Then always comes a mighty shudder

Through the day I hide it well
I tend to hide in my shell

Very quiet as I enter school
But also, I know to follow a rule

In the line, I now do stand
With all this sweat dripping down my hand

I'll be fine, I say in my head
I can cope with this but I really dread

3:15 comes and I am fine
To that safe place I head and that is mine

I often get pain at night
The panic sets in
The tears I cry, I think I'll die

By the end of each day
I'm glad I faced my fears
But most of the time, it ends in tears.

Chloe Gibson (12)
Woodham Academy, Newton Aycliffe

I'm Still Here

Look into the corner
I'm still here
I never left so do not shed a tear
We marched to war
All joyous and fun
But that did not last when we heard the sound of the gun
The thump of my chest
I felt my mouth drying
Nothing to hear but grown men crying

Across the field of ice and snow
Over the top, we had to go
We marched into hell, myself and others
Fathers, sons, uncles and brothers
We fell to the ground
Like newly-mown hay
In the hope to be found by the end of the day
But we were alone
With no one around
Nothing to see, not even a sound

A flash, a bang, my world became red
My friend called to his mother, but then he was dead
I stared to the sky and I started crying
I couldn't move, even though I was trying
My world grew dark
My life ebbed away

I'm still in the place that I died that day
I wait for my mother
While I shed a tear
I wait for my mother
I've always been here.

Sienna Birkett (12)
Woodham Academy, Newton Aycliffe

Mother Nature

It's sad to say but our mother is dying
So of her gifts, we must stop relying
We've massacred her pets and ravaged her garden
Now her discipline is beginning to harden

She's given fair warning, killing millions with ease
Using flood, famine and disease
We must act now before nothing is left
Except pain, suffering and regret

We must realize her resources will run out
Even if it's 100 years or thereabout
We can start now, it's not too late
To stop the carnage we create

If we replace the trees and stop the wars
It can be like it was before
Lush, green lands where animals roam free
We need to stop the anger and greed
If we change one thing at a time
Off her deathbed, our mother may climb.

Callum Hayden James McBride (12)
Woodham Academy, Newton Aycliffe

The Death Of An Animal

Soft, sweet swaying of trees in an empty patch of land
The lion reigning over his subject - big, bold, grand
While survival of the fittest at work once again
As the lion eats the deer of which he has just slain

The death of an animal for survival

A circus filled with joyous, cruel human beings
Watching a dancing lion, not acknowledging its feelings
Not knowing the terror as its parents were killed
Their wish of protecting him could never be fulfilled

The death of an animal for entertainment

What gives us the right to kill animals for fun?
Why can't we appreciate them in the long run?
Animals are living with a heart and a brain
If you can't accept that, you are to blame.

Mollie Marsh (12)
Woodham Academy, Newton Aycliffe

Grandad

Grandad, I love you with all my heart
I love you to the moon and back
Even if you're not here once I'm old
You can love me whilst I bloom

Grandad, please don't be sad
We do the best we can for you
And hope you will be glad
We brought your favourite liquorice

Even if you're worried
Even if you're sad
Even if you're bothered
Even if you're mad

Take your time to take a break
As even you may not have a lifetime
Nor a second in the world
To stay with the ones you cherish

However, try your best to make him blessed
With all the time he may have left
As even he may know
He may soon have to leave and go.

Ben Cole Graham (14)
Woodham Academy, Newton Aycliffe

Think

Think about your actions, are you throwing away food?
Why don't you just stop and think about how people feel?
Empty stomachs, crying in pain, stomachs rumbling
So many people in this world have nothing
And you're wasting food
Someone else could have eaten it
To stop hungry kids and adults
Stop people crying because the pain is unbearable
Stop people's stomachs aching
So, when you're eating food
And you're about to throw it away
Stop and think about all those people
Who could be starving
Because they can't get proper meals like us
And they don't even have money to buy food
So remember, stop and think!

Chelsea Allen (12)
Woodham Academy, Newton Aycliffe

What Would Happen If We Cared For Our Nature?

All these years
We've never noticed
But stand for a moment
And see us shine
If only you just had a little more time
Then you could have a chance

We would stand tall
If you cared
But you never have
We're always here, every day
But do you care?
We will never know

The hope we have
Might not show
But we are waiting for you to care
We look at you as you walk by
And see you cry
But stop for a moment
And have a look
And we will brighten up your day!

What would happen if you cared?
We will never know

Just care for nature
And you will see
What will happen if you care for nature!

Katie Heyburn (11)
Woodham Academy, Newton Aycliffe

John's Last Chapter

My life was like a ride
But suddenly, all my hope died
It was like a storm
Like my insides were torn
My neck leaked
And my legs stiffened
I panicked
I couldn't taste anything
The pain came and went
But my pain's never been spent
It all came to me like thunder
I felt my heart wonder
The Enfermera called my name
My hearing drifted away
All I could hear was my heartbeat leaving
But everything was still proceeding
I could never forgive the pain I was given
Therefore, it was my time to go to heaven
I'm so sorry, but today's the day all my sorrows drift away...

Ellie Taylor (14)
Woodham Academy, Newton Aycliffe

Pure Blood

I want to go home
I want to be free
You have trapped me here only to torture me
I am your entertainment
My cries bring you joy
You tore out my teeth and claws
Now, I shall die
My blood is pure
I am alive
Why can't you understand
I'm not a toy

My heart is heavy
Fear runs through my veins
As you approach my cage
I just want to escape
You place my feet on burning coals
And watch me dance
You take control
I fell faint with all the pain
Yet, all I hear
Is laughing people and heartless souls cheer

I am not a toy!

Scarlett Jean Liddle (11)
Woodham Academy, Newton Aycliffe

Litter

Rubbish everywhere
No bin
We will chuck it anywhere
Paper notes blow
Broken bottles scattered everywhere
The Earth depends on your actions
Take the time to make it fine
Each blade of grass, every animal in its nature
Endangered animals, injured, hurt
It's as though World War Three has just begun
Every piece of litter you throw is hurting the Earth
But not as you know
Drains blocked, lives lost
Polluted land, litter-covered seas
Making it so a party began in the ocean
The Earth is not able to fight day and night.

Jamie Porter (12)
Woodham Academy, Newton Aycliffe

Documents Of The Past

They turned, remembering the memories that shook them
They took her thoughts, documents of the past
They took a step, shaking at the memories that haunted them
Her thoughts, documents of the past
They dreamt, trying to forget the memories that drove them mad
Thoughts, documents of the past

Documents of the past

The memories that shook them
The memories that haunted them
The memories that drove them mad
The memories that were not theirs

Documents of the past.

Emily Sowels (14)
Woodham Academy, Newton Aycliffe

Children In Need

Once again, it's that time of year
Pudsey Bear is finally here
Donate some money to show you care
How would you feel if your family lived out there?

Struggling to survive
Every day a battle to stay alive
Your children cry for some food to eat
Anything to keep going that little heartbeat

So on this special night
Make sure these children get a good, long fight
At a good life that we know
Come on, let your love show.

Courtney Harker (11)
Woodham Academy, Newton Aycliffe

Sunshine

It was a brilliant day
The sun was shining
And the children were playing

Until the clouds took over
And the rain started to pour
I hate those days
When the sun stops bringing joy

I feel like I'm going to cry
When the rain hits the floor
What else is there to do
Except be bored?

If the rain stops
We can have some fun
But if it drizzles some more
We'll have to be bored.

Kacey Britton (11)
Woodham Academy, Newton Aycliffe

Nothing New Here!

Up and down,
Down and up,
Nothing new here.

Burned skin,
Blistered back,
Nothing new here.

Bruised arms,
Long whip,
Nothing new here.

Skinny slaves,
No food,
Nothing new here.

Sore throats,
Broken hearts,
Nothing new here.

Lucy Grayson (12)
Woodham Academy, Newton Aycliffe

YOUNG WRITERS INFORMATION

We hope you have enjoyed reading this book – and that you will continue to in the coming years.

If you're a young writer who enjoys reading and creative writing, or the parent of an enthusiastic poet or story writer, do visit our website **www.youngwriters.co.uk**. Here you will find free competitions, workshops and games, as well as recommended reads, a poetry glossary and our blog. There's lots to keep budding writers motivated to write!

If you would like to order further copies of this book, or any of our other titles, then please give us a call or visit **www.youngwriters.co.uk**.

Young Writers
Remus House
Coltsfoot Drive
Peterborough
PE2 9BF
(01733) 890066
info@youngwriters.co.uk

Join in the conversation!
Tips, news, giveaways and much more!

YoungWritersUK @YoungWritersCW